DID YOU KNOW?

TURKEYS STRIKE OUT

and other fun facts

To Lydia: I'm so excited! We're going to New York!
—A. S.

LITTLE SIMON
An imprint of Simon & Schuster Children's Publishing Division
1230 Avenue of the Americas, New York, New York 10020
This Little Simon edition March 2016
Series concept by Laura Lyn DiSiena
Copyright © 2016 by Simon & Schuster, Inc.
For information about special discounts for bulk purchases, please contact Simon & Schuster Special Sales at 1-866-506-1949 or business@simonandschuster.com.
The Simon & Schuster Speakers Bureau can bring authors to your live event. For more information or to book an event, contact the Simon & Schuster Speakers Bureau at 1-866-248-3049 or visit our website at www.simonspeakers.com.
Designed by Ciara Gay
Manufactured in China 0116 SCP
10 9 8 7 6 5 4 3 2 1
Library of Congress Cataloging-in-Publication Data
Names: Eliot, Hannah. | Spurgeon, Aaron, ill.
Title: Turkeys strike out / by Hannah Eliot ; illustrated by Aaron Spurgeon.
Description: First Edition. | New York : LITTLE SIMON, [2016] |
Series: Did You Know? ; 9 | Includes bibliographical references and index.
Identifiers: LCCN 2015023880 | ISBN 9781481451680 (pbk : alk. paper) |
ISBN 9781481451697 (hc : alk. paper) | ISBN 9781481451703 (eBook)
Subjects: LCSH: Sports—Miscellanea—Juvenile literature.
Classification: LCC GV707 .E44 2016 | DDC 796—dc23
LC record available at http://lccn.loc.gov/2015023880

DID YOU KNOW?

TURKEYS STRIKE OUT

and other fun facts

By Hannah Eliot

Illustrated by Aaron Spurgeon

LITTLE SIMON

New York   London   Toronto   Sydney   New Delhi

Oh! Hey there! Do you know the song "Take Me Out to the Ball Game"? Did you know that it's usually sung in the middle of the seventh inning of a baseball game? What else do you know about baseball?

How about that baseball cards have been around since 1869? And that only 16 major-league players have ever hit 4 home runs in a single game? Did you know that a "meatball" is an easy pitch to hit?

Wait, you knew ALL of those things? Well . . . did you know that TURKEYS STRIKE OUT?

It's not because turkeys are bad at baseball. It's because "turkey" is another name for 3 strikes in a row in BOWLING! A strike is when you knock down all 10 pins on your first try. WOW! There's evidence that bowling originated in ancient Egypt, more than 5,000 years ago. Today bowling is a fun activity for all ages. Even the president of the United States gets to bowl! A bowling alley was first installed at the White House in 1947 as a gift for President Harry S. Truman. In 1969, President Richard Nixon installed a new one-lane alley for himself. The very first indoor bowling lanes were built in London in 1455. And the largest bowling alley in the world is Japan's Inazawa Grand Bowl.

Baseball is the most popular sport in Japan based on the amount of people who play *and* watch it.

In Australia, cricket is popular.

In Canada, ice hockey is.

In China, table tennis is played a lot.

But the most popular sport in the WORLD is . . . SOCCER!

That's right. It's the most attended or watched sport of all of them. Did you know that soccer is actually called football in almost every country *except* the United States and Canada? The World Cup is a soccer tournament held every 4 years since 1930, and the 20 FIFA World Cup tournaments have been won by 8 different national teams. Brazil has won the most—5 times! The other winners are Italy, Germany, Argentina, Uruguay, England, France, and Spain. The women's World Cup was established in 1991. Want to know something interesting? A 2-0 score is the most frequent result in the Women's World Cup. In the men's tournament, a 1-0 score is the most common! The highest score ever made in *any* soccer game was 149-0. GOOOOAL!

Soccer players wear shin guards to protect themselves from the ball and other players' cleats. Other sports *also* require shin guards. Hockey—both on the ice and on the field—is one of them! Hockey is the oldest-known ball-and-stick game. Did you know that *all* field hockey sticks are right-handed? Or that men's field hockey has the FASTEST swing speed of any sport—faster than baseball and golf?

The first indoor ice hockey game was played in Montreal in 1875. Today, professional ice rinks contain a layer of ice that's about an inch thick and kept at 15.8 degrees Fahrenheit. Ice hockey players wear lots of other equipment besides shin guards. They wear ice skates, too. Can you name the main difference between a hockey skate and a figure skate? It's that hockey skates don't have a toe pick!

The purpose of a toe pick is that it allows skaters to do amazing JUMPS and SPINS! There are two main categories of jumps in figure skating. There are toe jumps, such as the toe loop, the flip, and the Lutz. And there are edge jumps, such as the Salchow and the Axel. Some categories of spins are: camel spin, sit spin, and upright spin. Did you know that figure skating was first included in the *Summer* Olympics in 1908, but since 1924 it has been included as a Winter Olympic sport?

BOBSLEDDING. SPEED SKATING. and CURLING are some other sports performed on ice. Bobsledding is a sport in which teams of 2 or 4 people race down a narrow, twisting ice track in a sled that's powered only by gravity. Each team's run is timed—that's how a winner is determined. The sport was named "bobsled" because the members of a team "bob" back and forth in the sled to increase its speed. Bobsleds can go up to nearly 100 miles per hour!

Skiing is another popular winter activity. Skis used to be made of only wood, but these days they are made using a combination of materials, including plastic foams and fiberglass. On a ski mountain, trails are marked according to their level of difficulty. A green circle marks the easiest, a blue square is for an intermediate trail, a black diamond means the trail is for advanced skiers, and a DOUBLE BLACK DIAMOND is for experts only.

Did you know that astronauts have noticed that the moon would make a great ski spot? That's right—there's a place on the moon called the Sea of Serenity that has a mountainous rim perfect for skiing! And downhill skiing isn't the only way to get down a mountain. Freestyle skiing involves acrobatic moves such as flips and jumps, and it can include moguls, ramps, and half-pipes as well!

So are you REGULAR, or are you GOOFY? No, not right now! When you snowboard! See, "regular" means you snowboard with your left foot forward, and "goofy" means you snowboard with your right foot forward. The modern snowboard was created in 1965 when a man named Sherman Poppen invented a toy by tying two skis together. He called this a "Snurfer"—a combination of "snow" and "surfer"!

BRRRR! Enough about winter sports! Does snowboarding remind you of anything else? Maybe . . . surfing? Surfing has probably been around as long as humans have been swimming in the ocean. What we know as surfing today originated in Hawaii. Some of the best places to surf include: Pipeline in Oahu, Hawaii; Supertubes in Jeffrey's Bay, South Africa; and Uluwatu and Kuta in Bali, Indonesia.

OAHU, HAWAII

JEFFREY'S BAY, SOUTH AFRICA

BALI, INDONESIA

Get ready to BUMP, SET, and SPIKE! Volleyball is another activity you might see at a beach. Volleyball is played with 6 players on each side of a court—or beach—separated by a net. Teams score points by hitting the ball onto the ground on the other team's side. Some games related to volleyball include Buka Ball (volleyball played only with the feet!) and Newcomb ball (where the ball is caught and then thrown, rather than hit). Do you know what an "ace" in volleyball is? Just like in tennis, it's when a ball is served to the other team and no one touches it. How about a "dig"? That's when a player makes an awesome save after their opponent has spiked the ball down!

Ace, dig . . . There are lots of sports terms out there. Some may be familiar—such as "kickoff," "slam dunk," and "home run." But some terms and phrases might surprise you!

Do you know what a "can of corn" is in baseball? It's an easy catch made by a fielder. HA!

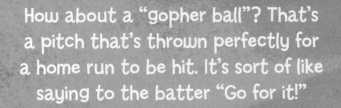

How about a "gopher ball"? That's a pitch that's thrown perfectly for a home run to be hit. It's sort of like saying to the batter "Go for it!"

In soccer, a "bicycle kick" is when a player jumps into the air and kicks the ball over and behind his head!

In basketball, a "granny shot" is an underhand shot using both hands.

In water polo, players kick their feet back and forth to keep afloat. This is called an "eggbeater" kick!

There are other important parts of basketball besides granny shots and slam dunks, you know. When basketball was invented in 1891, the first "hoops" ever made were just peach baskets! And the first basketball was brown, not orange.

Peaches

According to the basketball manufacturer Spalding, the average life span of an NBA basketball is 10,000 bounces.

Did you know that if you are **7 FEET TALL** or taller you have a 17% chance of playing in the NBA? How about that the Boston Celtics have won more NBA championships than any other team? They've won 17! Did you know that the Los Angeles Lakers started as the Detroit Gems? That's right—Detroit, Michigan! They then moved to Minneapolis, Minnesota, where they were renamed the "Lakers" to reflect the Minnesota state nickname "Land of 10,000 Lakes." Finally they ended up in Los Angeles.

The Lakers don't have a team mascot, but other teams sure do. The Chicago Bulls have Benny the Bull, the Houston Rockets have Clutch the Rockets Bear, the Phoenix Suns have the Suns Gorilla, and the Atlanta Hawks have Harry the Hawk.

Mascots can be an important part of a sports team! A mascot is typically a person, animal, or object thought to bring good luck to a team. One well-known mascot is Mr. Met, the mascot for the New York Mets baseball team. In fact, he has been called the number 1 mascot of *all* sports! Maybe he should be called Mr. Popular!

Do you know what the mascot of the Colorado Rockies is? A purple triceratops named Dinger! He became the team mascot because during the construction of the Rockies' stadium, Coors Field, DINOSAUR FOSSILS were found—including a rib fragment of a dinosaur near home plate.

You won't find many mascots hanging around tennis courts. Tennis is mostly an individual sport, not a team sport. Modern tennis has been around since the late 1800s, when it was called lawn tennis! Today the game can be played on different types of surfaces. Some are: clay, grass, carpet, and wood. The four Grand Slam tournaments in tennis are Wimbledon, Roland Garros (the French Open), the Australian Open, and the US Open. Historically, a tennis ball was either black or white. But in 1972, yellow tennis balls were introduced because they are more visible on TV!

Here are some fun Wimbledon facts:

The fastest serve recorded in that tournament was 148 miles per hour.

SERVE SPEED 148 MPH

Each year about 350,000 cups of tea and coffee are served to tournament attendees . . .

and 15,000 bananas are given to the players!

And did you know that 290 MILLION tennis balls would fit into Centre Court?

Footballs are bigger than tennis balls, and a different shape. The football shape is called a prolate spheroid, but you might just call it football-shaped! When you think of football, you might think of the SUPER BOWL. That's because it's the most watched television event in the United States! There's a joke that during Super Bowl halftime, there are 90 million toilet flushes! That's equal to 180 million gallons of water flowing at once, OR 3.5 minutes of flowing water from Niagara Falls!

Although football games last about 3 hours, the ball is usually in play for an average of only 11 minutes. Have you ever seen a player do a dance after they score a touchdown? This is called a "touchdown celebration." A New York Giants player named Homer Jones is thought to have been the first one to celebrate after scoring, in a 1965 game, when he spiked the ball into the ground.

In 1954, the Baltimore Colts formed the first NFL cheerleading squad. Cheerleading requires a great deal of athleticism. And many cheerleaders are gymnasts as well. Cheerleading started out as an all-male sport, but today a much larger percentage of cheerleaders are female. One of the most recognizable cheerleading stunts is the pyramid. GO, TEAM!

Golf doesn't require the same flexibility that cheerleading does, but it does require strength! Did you know that most golf balls have between 300 and 500 dimples on them? The dimples allow the ball to fly farther! Do you know what else helps a golf ball travel far? Heat! When it's warmer out, that means the air is less dense than when it's cold, so the ball can travel farther.

Did you know that even though the MOON apparently would be great for skiing, golf is one of two sports that have actually been *played* there? In 1971, astronaut Alan Shepard hit 2 golf balls on the moon! You've probably heard of a "hole in one" before—when a player gets their golf ball in the hole on their first shot! For professional golfers, the chances of getting a hole in one are 1 in 2,500. For amateur golfers, the chances are 1 in 12,500! Better start practicing!

By the way, the other sport performed on the moon was a javelin throw!

One thing athletes surely practice and train for is the Olympics. The Olympics can be traced back to 776 BC in ancient Greece. That's nearly 3,000 years ago! At that time, Greek athletes performed NAKED! They did this to show off their muscles and to show the Greek god Zeus how they had trained their bodies. In the beginning, there was only one event at the Olympics—a footrace. The first ever winner was a chef named Coroebus. The first official Olympic games hosted by the International Olympic Committee, however, were in 1896 in Athens, Greece. Today there are 28 sports included in the summer Olympics and 15 in the winter Olympics.

Did you know that the game of tug-of-war was an Olympic sport from 1900 to 1920?

And do you know what the five rings on the Olympic flag symbolize? They symbolize Africa, Asia, Australia, Europe, and the Americas.

Did you know that GOLD MEDALS aren't *actually* made of gold? They're silver with gold plating over them!

Winning isn't everything, but medals and trophies are pretty cool! Since ancient times, trophies have marked wins. Trophies can come in the form of cups or in the form of statues of humans, animals, or objects . . . and more.

The World Cup trophy for soccer is of two figures holding up the earth.

The Heisman Trophy is awarded to the best player in college football.

The Stanley Cup is a trophy nearly 3 feet tall that's awarded to the winner of the National Hockey League play-offs. It's engraved with the names of the winning players and coaches.

The Tour de France, one of the biggest bicycle races in the world, awards a yellow bike jersey to the winner.

WORL WINNER

In baseball, the biggest tournament is the World Series.
The winning team gets the Commissioner's Trophy.
And unlike turkeys, that team sure doesn't STRIKE OUT!

MORE FUN FACTS

Soccer: Until 1875, there were no crossbars on soccer goals. This means that any ball that went in between the two side posts at *any* height was considered a goal.

Baseball: Every MLB baseball is rubbed with mud to take off the shiny gloss the factory puts on it.

Olympics: Women were not allowed to participate in the Olympics until 1900. Today nearly half of the Olympic athletes are women.

Surfing: The annual Surf City Surf Dog contest—where dogs compete on surfboards—takes place in California every year.

Bowling: If you get 6 strikes in a row, you've got a "wild turkey." And if you get 9 strikes, you've got a "golden turkey"!

Figure skating: In synchronized skating, 8 to 20 figure skaters move as a team, performing tricks and footwork in sync!

Trophies: Sometimes a trophy comes in the form of a ring! Some of the best-known rings are the NBA championship ring, the NFL's Super Bowl ring, MLB's World Series ring, and the NHL's Stanley Cup ring.

Skiing: Revelstoke Mountain Resort has the longest vertical drop in North America—more than 1 mile!

Ice hockey: A Zamboni is a machine used to clear the ice in an ice rink.

Basketball: Dunking was banned in the NCAA from 1967–1976.

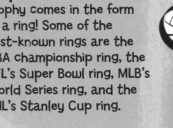

Volleyball: Volleyball is called this because players "volley" the ball back and forth over the net.

Mascots: There are Olympic mascots too! The mascot is supposed to represent the culture of the host city where the Olympics are being held that year.

Tennis: Tennis may have originated from a French game that was played using hands, not rackets!

Football: A football field is 57,600 square feet!

Golf: Until golf balls had solid cores, they had liquid ones—and that liquid was often *honey*!